How to Stop for A Cop

Reconnecting Law Enforcement & The Community

Thank you Don for
all your Love & Support

How to Stop for A Cop

Reconnecting Law Enforcement & The Community

Sheriff Hubert A. Peterkin

Former President of The North Carolina Sheriff's Assoc.
Chairman of The N.C. Sheriff's Assoc, Executive Board

Copyright

Printed in the United States of America.

First Printing,

ISBN-13: 978-1-947656-48-2
ISBN10: 1947656481

The Butterfly Typeface Publishing
PO BOX 56193
Little Rock Arkansas 72215
www.butterflytypeface.com
info@butterflytypeface.com

Dedication

I dedicate this book to my very first love. When I met this woman, as she smiled at me I knew without a doubt that I had entered into a relationship of love that would last a lifetime. She is the first woman that ever touched me, held me, and gave me my first kiss. No one forgets that first hug and kiss. In a relationship everyone needs that special someone who truly cares for them and unselfishly gives their all.

Just like any relationship, my first love and I had our tensed moments where communication was broken and even trust at times, but she never stopped loving me. Often times I would express to her my goals and my dreams and she would encourage me to press on to do my best.

It is strange to be married and find time to slip away to spend time with that very first special someone that loved and loves you unconditionally'. I hope those who read this book can forgive me for loving another woman and if you can't please don't judge me because everyone of us have or are doing just what I am doing and that is loving their mother.

So without hesitation I dedicate this book to the first woman I ever loved, my 77 year old mommy, Ms. Onnie B. Peterkin.

"Let's Stay Alive"

The number one rule is that everyone safely goes home from a traffic stop!

Hubert A. Peterkin

Contents

Foreword

I have personally and professionally known Sheriff Peterkin for many years. When I was elected the Sheriff of Richmond County in 2010 Pete was assigned by the North Carolina Sheriff's Association to mentor me as a new Sheriff. The bond between us was magical.

Sheriff Peterkin is an experienced officer, leader and a proven professional with over 30 years in his law enforcement career'. With much passion he recently expressed to me that he was writing a book titled, "How To Stop For A Cop". I immediately realized the need for the information and content that this book contains. This book unlike similar books addresses persons of all cultures, status, and ages.

Sheriff Peterkin captures the imagination, and concerns that we hear about and read about throughout the communities we serve. I often tell other leaders in Law Enforcement that the **Fear is real**. Restoring the public trust is an immediate issue in the State of North Carolina and other states. It is imperative that Law Enforcement and the Community come back to a point of togetherness as it relates to traffic stops. Pete reminds all Law Enforcement of what they stand for and how important training accountability, and focusing on the ethics, integrity, and simply doing the right thing in a traffic stop could prevent a serious injury or fatal outcome.

In addition to this he emphasizes the importance of community respect and cooperation when stopped by an officer. In this book you will learn what is expected by you when you are stopped and understand what you should expect from an officer. With given examples Peterkin reflects on real incidents and gives law enforcement and the community a positive message to ensure a positive outcome no matter what. As the Elected

Sheriff of Richmond County and the First Vice President of the North Carolina Sheriff's Association I see this book titled "How To Stop For A Cop" as a tool for guiding, learning, and teaching all readers, organizations, churches, schools, colleges, and driver training for new drivers. This book will argue Sheriff Peterkin's perspective and satisfy his goal to regain the public trust and reunite Law Enforcement and the community.

Sheriff James E. Clemons Jr.

Acknowledgments

This book could not have been written without the help and advice of many people. First let me start with the support of my family. I want to thank my wife Della who read my drafts, corrected my directions, commented on photos, and encouraged me to write this book.

I want to thank my nephew Aaron Lide Jr. for his valuable input, ideas, and motivation. I want to express my appreciation to the following professionals who provided invaluable assistance:

First Lt. Mark Caskey who is the Training Coordinator and Patrol Lieutenant for the Hoke County Sheriff's Office. Mark gave me his full attention and pointed me in the right direction.

Second, I want to thank Ms. Thomasema Pannell for her valuable advice and input. Thomasema is the writer and author of "Denton Place Tables Turned" (Books 1&2).

I want to also thank Richmond County Sheriff James E. Clemmons for his support and friendship and Rockingham County Sheriff Sam Page for giving me further insight on governmental concerns and initiatives.

I want to acknowledge career law enforcement and personal mentors:

Law Enforcement:

Dr. Sam Pearson (Retired Lieutenant, Fayetteville Police Department), Gary Porter (Former Investigator and Training Officer, Fayetteville Police Department), and Ron Snyder, (Retired Lieutenant, Fayetteville Police Department)

Personal Mentors:

Dr. Milton H. Williams Sr. who has inspired my life since childhood, Mr. Parnell Miles an encourager, mentor, and friend, the late Stan Callender Sr., one of the greatest Hoke County Basketball Coaches of all time, the late Mr. Raz Autry, former Hoke County Schools Superintendent and former Campaign Manager, Mr. Don Steed, former Hoke County Schools Superintendent and current Campaign Manager, and the late Bob Gentry, former Mayor of Raeford, and longtime friend.

A very special thanks to my wonderful Pastor the Reverend Dr. Christopher Stackhouse Sr. for his prayers and spiritual guidance throughout the writing process and to Overseer Artie McPhatter; like a mother she has always cared and prayed for me and most of all she blessed this book from the beginning as I wrote it.

Preface

Looking back over my career as a patrol officer, I remember the sigh of relief of a victim when I would arrive on the scene of a hostile situation.

There was a great appreciation for what the man or woman behind the badge stood for and our presence was welcomed with open arms and with much trust. The communication was open and respectful even during traffic stops.

Today in the 21st century there is a serious disconnect between law enforcement and the community. There are consistent shootings involving cops shooting persons or persons shooting cops, particularly doing traffic stops.

Many of these traffic stops involve white cops shooting black males or altercations between officers and black males that lead to unexplained injuries or deaths throughout the United States.

I must make one thing clear as I write this book; the only side that I am on, is the side of right and not wrong.

A lot of the content in this book is based on over 30 years of experience, which consists of my training, observation, management, leadership, and my opinion. Every person has one.

There are circumstances where in my opinion the officers have been wrong in their actions and there have been circumstances where the person pursued was wrong or the contributions of both the officer and the driver led to unexpected injuries or a fatal outcome.

Two wrongs can't make it right.

There is one thing I know to be true and that is that law enforcement officers need the community and the community needs law enforcement. In short, right is right and wrong is wrong and at the end of the day we simply need each other.

So, the question becomes how do we fix this serious disconnect between law enforcement and the community today? How do we as law enforcement officers restore the public trust?

It is my belief that until the blame game has changed, all of the finger pointing has stopped, and there is a willingness to seriously sit down at the table to talk, plan, educate, and strategize with all the necessary persons this problem will continue to escalate.

Every situation that we are now reading about or see on TV usually starts with a cop stopping a person whether it is in a car or a face-to-face approach. I believe that if both the cop and driver do what is right during a traffic stop the end result would be totally different from most of the sad stories we are reading about today.

This book, "*How to Stop for a Cop*" is comprised of a step by step guide on how to stop for a cop and public safety information with the intent to reconnect all law enforcement and the community with a defined message for each throughout the book.

Introduction

When I was six years old I was laying on the couch just before 11 PM and my mother came over to wake me up to go to bed. As I sat up on the couch the TV was still playing, and the news was on. They had just announced that Dr. Martin Luther King Jr. had been killed. The broadcast began to show all the great things that he had done and how he had helped so many black people as well as people of other cultures as he fought for equality. I could hear my mother and father talking with great concern and hurt for what had just happened. I remember asking my mother why would someone want to kill this man if he had done so much good and she stated to me that there are a lot of bad people in the world who do bad things. I also remember wishing that I could have done something to help him and I was only six years old. I thought about what a wonderful feeling it would be to be able to help those who needed help from the bad guys. By the time I reached the age of ten I had made up my mind that I wanted to be a cop. Every day I dreamed about saving lives and protecting people and I would tell my mother so many times over and over again that one day I'm going to be a cop and even though she did everything she could to discourage me because she was afraid of me getting hurt I knew deep down inside that one day this would be my calling.

Today as I write this book *"How to Stop for a Cop"* I am serving over 30 years in law enforcement. As I dreamed of one day doing this **I always looked at cops as the good guys taking care of people, protecting people, being kind to people, loving people, and showing the citizens that we protect that we were there for them no matter what without any bias, discrimination, or fear.**

In my mind we're like brothers and sisters fighting crime loving one another from within as we put our lives on the line to do what was needed and what is right all the time.

Chapter One
Why Are Ethics Important?

The Law enforcement profession has traditionally been viewed as a pedestal profession. Our community holds law enforcement to very high standards and expects leaders and officers to always show a conduct that is moral and right. I must remind citizens that officers are human too and deal with the same weaknesses and emotions as any other person. For the most part recommendations and references from the general public assist with the selection process but this is not an excuse for officers to not stay focused or let their guards down. The primary function of law enforcement is to maintain law and order in their assigned jurisdiction. In addition to this police officers are the first responders to a criminal situation and must decide if an arrest is necessary. Using discretion is not a new process and in some situations such as traffic stops, officers may use discretion in how they deal with drivers during the stop. Officers have used the decision to charge or to make an arrest for many years, however since discretionary laws have been established many questions and concerns have been made about the ethics, and morals in the decision-making. Each law enforcement officer is given an oath to swear or affirm to. The oath pledges a commitment and dedication to the citizens they serve and to enforce the laws of North Carolina or the state or jurisdiction they are in.

Officers must remember their oath of office and grasp the meaning of their oath from the very first day on the job. Embracing the ethics in a law enforcement career, leads officers to always do what is right and display the professionalism and the right attitude needed to protect and serve citizens in the community regardless of status or cultures. Lastly, I always encourage officers to occasionally take a personal inventory or self-evaluation of their personal ethics. This gives them a better awareness of their own moral standing, so they may consider this information when issues present themselves, especially during a traffic stop.

Law Enforcement Oath:

Hoke County Deputy Sheriff

"I, _____, do solemnly (swear)(or affirm) that I will support and maintain the Constitution and laws of the United States, and the Constitution and laws of North Carolina not inconsistent therewith, and that I will faithfully discharge the duties of my office as a Deputy Sheriff, so help me God."

"I, _____, do solemnly and sincerely swear or affirm that I will support the Constitution of the United States; that I will be faithful and bear true allegiance to the State of North Carolina, and to the constitutional powers and authorities which are or may be established for the government thereof; and that I will endeavor to support, maintain and defend the Constitution of said State, not inconsistent with the Constitution of the United States, to the best of my knowledge and ability; so help me God."

"I, _____, so solemnly swear (or affirm) that I will be alert and vigilant to enforce the criminal laws of this State; that I will not be influenced in any manner on account of personal bias or prejudice; that I will faithfully and impartially execute the duties of my office as a law enforcement officer according to the best of my skill, abilities, and judgment; so help me, God."

_____

Deputy Sheriff

How to Stop for a Cop

Reflection: During my first year as a law enforcement officer with the Fayetteville Police Department I was patrolling one of the city streets in town. As I approached a yellow caution light I suddenly struck the car in front of me in the rear. I quickly jumped out and ran to the window of the driver.

"Are you okay sir?" I shouted.

The elderly gentleman stated, "Yes **I think so**."

I looked at him and advised him that his car looked okay as well. I went back to my car and left the scene. I kept the accident to myself, the patrol car, and the clouds above. Two weeks later Lt. Clarence Ware who was the Watch Commander on duty called me into his office. He looks at me and says, "Peterkin did you have an accident a few weeks ago and did not report it?"

My mouth dropped.

He immediately says, "Please don't lie to me.

Peterkin think about what you are going to say before you say it."

I confessed. He quickly advised me that I had not followed the accident policy and stated that he had received a complaint and that I was under investigation for failing to report an accident.

I received a written reprimand and later placed on a six-month probation which meant termination if another incident occurred during that time frame.

My actions were unethical because I failed to do the right thing by not reporting a direct violation of the departmental policy.

Message To Law Enforcement: Always do the right thing especially when we know better. Remember we live in a fish bowl and all eyes are on us. When we are out there don't ever think that what we do wrong won't catch up with us, trust me it will. As my mother used to say what you do in the dark will come to the light.

Message To The Community: I humbly ask our community to always use the complaint process when you believe an officer has wronged you. I can assure you that the upper leadership and command wants the best for you and will not tolerate unethical behavior from their officers. The process may not move as fast as you wish but it will pay off in the end.

Chapter Two
Supervision & Accountability

In this chapter when I think about supervision and accountability, there is one phrase that comes to mind and that is **everything starts from the top.** In my opinion there is absolutely no way that everything can go the way it should go and be done to the best of its ability without the proper supervision. In the business of law enforcement there is always a person or supervisor who is in charge at the top. It is important that leaders surround themselves with other competent managers or supervisors who can ensure that everything is being done correctly and handled properly. Throughout the organization ethics, morals, values, and integrity are needed and must be maintained. Every law-enforcement agency whether it is local or state is governed by a set of rules and regulations policies and procedures that must be updated frequently to be in accordance with state laws that may change. Trust me they do change.

What I have learned as the leader of a sheriff's office and managing, no matter how many rules and regulations or policies and procedures you learn, teach, or supply your officers with it is not enough to overcome the challenges of distrust, dislike, and unanswered questions that our community now has. I believe that all leaders of organizations now must find the time to get in front of their officers and their staff to talk to them about the importance of doing the right thing all time and being affective as it relates to the community. I have found this to be encouraging and rewarding in the end.

When I started my career in 1987 law enforcement focused more on addressing the relationship between themselves and kids. This was to ensure that kids grew up knowing that they could trust the police and not to be afraid of officers when they saw them. Law-enforcement agencies started investing in coloring books, pencils, sticker badges, and all types of little gifts for the children in hopes to win over their confidence and trust. This was better known as officer friendly and it worked. Today we find ourselves faced with a different challenge. The audience that we now need to address that we cannot win over with the checklist above is adults within the community, teenage drivers, and adult drivers. **As law-enforcement supervisors we must make sure that whatever procedures or policies we have in place there is a way that we can measure the effectiveness of our duties and we cannot do it correctly if we only hear one side of the story or believe everything that our officers say or do.**

I have no doubt in my mind with over 30 years in this business that the majority of the officers and supervisors in this profession feel the same way that I do and are taking the necessary actions to hold their personnel accountable. With today's technology such as audio and video in car camera systems, and body camera systems officers in the field known as first responders can be held more accountable for their actions and the citizens as well. Almost every law enforcement organization large and small has a professional standard or internal affairs division that investigates all complaints or allegations of wrong doings that involves an officer.

The question that I always ask during an interview to hire new officers is "Why do you want to do this job?" This is a very important question because if you are not in the business of law-enforcement to respectfully protect, serve, and enforce the law then you are absolutely in the wrong interview. I often say to my officers that if you have prejudices and judgmental stereotypes that will cause you to be unfair or unethical towards those you may encounter during traffic stops or any form of business to please find another job. This job is not for you! **Good**

supervision and accountability is not in the business of covering up or hiding wrong doings of an officer.

Leadership has been widely studied over a long period of time, yet it remains an elusive phenomenon to understand and develop. Many leadership theories composed over the years have influenced leadership models designed to assist leaders in every profession. Leaders must understand the theories and models to become more effective in their leadership. The organizational structures of law enforcement agencies large and small have placed all managers regardless of rank in some type of leadership role. Each role comes with levels of liability that directly involves citizens or the officers.

Most communities have become diverse with residents 'of all cultures placing a demand for law enforcement agencies to mirror the same. Law Enforcement leaders must understand the different leadership models and be able to apply what they have learned in the workplace. Leadership must be observable and consistent on both personal and professional levels. As leaders we should always remember that leadership is an observable set of skills and abilities and can be learned. **As Leaders, let's set the stage and lead by example.**

The law-enforcement profession of today is not the same profession as 30 years ago. As time changes and challenges become more demanding, leaders and officers must improve and evolve especially during traffic stops. Today during traffic stops we never know what we will run into but regardless, as law enforcement officers we want to make absolutely sure we are safe, but professional in every way as well. **Leaders must stay focused while making the necessary choices and decisions to protect citizens, quality of life, and those persons who we serve within the community.**

New law enforcement officers must socialize

themselves into the law enforcement profession and always be mindful of the parameters set by the *Code of Ethics* and remember the commitments made through their oath of office.

Reflection: Over the course of my career I have worked with officers, met officers, and supervised officers in uniform who **displayed attitudes, arrogance, control, and a mindset of get them all and lock them all up.** This has happened under my supervision and racism was involved from both white and black officers. Yes I said it and I am not proud of it, but I am keeping it real and they no longer have a job! Every call they would get dispatched to or traffic stop usually ended up in a fight or confrontation. Wow! Unfortunately, this type of officer still exists today in our profession and must be weeded out. Roundup weed control can't get rid of this problem. **As I have previously stated in this book everything starts at the top. Supervisors and managers when we see smoke we need to**

look for the fire and put it out immediately or shall I make it plain, put the officer out, because trouble is on the way! This officer is a headliner and it will not read well. We must pay attention to the warning signs. I have counseled, disciplined, evaluated, and fired officers with a constant smoke pattern that consisted of these attitudes and my managers and I continue to keep an eye out for it. We must look and spot the red flags. There are enough of negative attitudes in the community and on the streets, but we do not want to be the spark or light the flame.

Message To Enforcement: **Leaders and managers please pay attention to the warnings that promote negative turnout and consist of negative attitudes over and over again, especially during traffic stops.** If you find yourself continuously investigating complaints on an officer for this please do not ignore it. There are avenues to treat the problem to assist the officer if the problem exists, such as professional counseling and anger management, but **when all else fails this job may not be for him.**

Message to The Community: First allow me to say to our communities that a positive relationship between law enforcement and the community is needed more today than ever. Our goal as leaders, managers, and officers are to ensure your safety first, but **in reality our strength comes from knowing that we are accepted and loved by those we serve and we are often reminded of this.**

In regard to officers who may display all the negatives mentioned, it is a must that **you stand firm, and   not engage the negative.** Report it over and over again until you get some attention. Each time an officer is investigated for negative behavior it should always be documented by his superiors and placed in his personnel file. Please don't tell yourself that it won't do any good to report it. I have heard this numerous times and this is not true.

Leadership Practice and Procedure

The need for law enforcement leaders to ensure officers are able to use professional judgment during traffic stops and special circumstances while minimizing the risks for bias or abuse is essential. The strength of law enforcement policies remains, but leaders need to wield such policies flexibly to allow the law enforcement officers to account for unique and unexpected situations during a traffic stop. Basically during traffic stops the officer needs to simply just think outside the box and maybe use a little discretion that could possibly prevent unnecessary confrontations that may lead to unwanted issues. Regardless of the leadership style, both integrity and knowledge are necessary to perform effectively. As I previously stated, having policies and procedures are fine but today I truly believe that leaders must find the quality time to talk and communicate with their managers as well as their officers to reiterate issues, concerns, dos, and don'ts.

This is a must!

Integrity

Integrity and knowledge is a dynamic human process of justifying personal belief toward the truth, information, or actions taken, especially when an officer executes his duties during a traffic stop. Trust me this is a very big responsibility. As stated, leaders must lead the officers they supervise by example.

Integrity is very important in law enforcement especially when it applies to Leadership. Integrity is identified as one of the characteristics of effective leadership related to higher levels of motivation and production from the officers they manage and lead. Integrity and knowledge form a dynamic human process justifying personal belief toward the truth or information.

In the law enforcement profession, leaders and officers cannot jeopardize the trust of others. We must focus and ensure that the integrity of our law enforcement duties does not rely on our individual beliefs but a combination of training, enforcing laws according to law, and do what is right all the time. Officers must continue to increase individual knowledge, research, and training.

Developing trust among employees and citizens requires leaders to demonstrate behaviors exhibiting integrity and consistency of control. Leaders who possess personal traits such as integrity, honesty, and trustworthiness align themselves with moral character, inspiring staff and persons that serve in the community, particularly when interacting with them during a traffic stop. Such ethics and trustworthiness consist of leading by example, credibility, predictability, and consistency, including respect and concern for all citizens and allowing the citizens to respectfully express issues and concerns during the traffic stop. The expressions should be very minimum and non-confrontational. If a driver has a complaint advise them of the formal complaint process.

Emotional Intelligence of Law Enforcement Officers

Research of law enforcement officers and leadership has included theories relating to emotional intelligence. Emotional intelligence is a set of multiple capabilities to perceive, manage, assess, and evaluate one's own and other persons' emotions; optimize personal potential and performance; manage relationships; develop social, economic, and political awareness; and improve social understanding and sociability. Emotional intelligence is the ability to monitor one's own and others' feelings and emotions, differentiating between them, and allowing the information to guide one's thinking and actions.

In law enforcement, another aspect of emotional intelligence is discretion. Officers who focus on personal innermost feelings when responding to calls or conducting traffic stops tend to exercise discretion to ensure the best outcome possible for the situation by eliminating personal biases. Emotional intelligence focuses on differentiating among emotions and using the differences to redirect thinking and actions, allowing problem solving by learning from and dealing with pleasant or unpleasant innermost feelings as emotions arrive instead of ignoring the feelings.

With regard to the emerging affective revolution in social and organizational environment, supporters propose emotional intelligence as an important predictor of key organizational outcomes, including job satisfaction. Evidence suggests emotional intelligence abilities and traits encourage job satisfaction, and employers need to select employees for positions or jobs that demand a high degree of social interaction. **In law enforcement, agencies should not and can't afford to hire officers with a hot head, a hunger for power, or anyone that does not understand the importance and need to build or retain good community relations.**

Each law enforcement situation is different, including traffic stops. Understanding the importance of emotional intelligence may eliminate over-aggressiveness or lack of cooperation from all persons involved.

Please allow me to outline four main components associated with emotional intelligence.

1. The first component is **self-awareness**, which involves leaders and officer's ability to read personal emotions and instincts to make decisions.
2. The second component is **self-management**, the ability to control personal emotions and adapt to changes as necessary, especially during a traffic stop.
3. The third component is **social awareness**, which requires the ability to not only understand personal emotions, but also to appropriately react to the emotions of others within the social contexts to include traffic stops.
4. The final component is **relationship management** or the ability to inspire, influence, and develop others to promote a positive outcome in any situation to include traffic stops.

Chapter Three
Community Policing

There has been numerous officer-involved shootings all across the United States that has become very controversial in every way. Most shootings have led to violence, riots, lootings, officer ambushes, and protest.

I must say that I became troubled by the circumstances that may have led to the officer's decision-making and sometimes actions of the driver, persons approached or pursued.

As this concern or problem appears to be growing each day, again I must say it is my belief that it will never get better or go away as long as the finger pointing between law enforcement and the community continues.

There has to be a serious meeting of the minds or this disconnect will continue.

It is time for law enforcement leaders, officers, community leaders, grassroots leaders, the faith base community, pastors, **teenage drivers**, etc. to sit down and be proactive to this problem and not only react to each situation when it occurs.

Across the United States, law enforcement agencies have implemented programs referred to as community policing, a proactive way to reduce crime, minimize issues, and builds public trust.

In addition community policing is a crime-fighting tool focused on reducing and managing rising crime rates throughout the community. Community policing programs date back as far as the late 1700s originally designed and developed by Robert Peel.

Peel created the first police department in London, England on the philosophy of community policing. Peel believed police and the public were synonymous, with the only difference as police officers being citizens of the public who received compensation for giving fulltime attention to the duties, which were incumbent on every citizen in the interest of the community safety and existence.

Law enforcement is an extension of the community and officers must work closely with the citizens. All community leaders and all leaders within the law enforcement profession need to identify the root of the problem as it relates to officer involved shootings during traffic stops and recognize the need for community policing regarding the distrust between them and the community. After officials and leaders identify the problem organized meetings must take place to communicate, share information, promote unity, and develop teamwork, as well as self-awareness and motivation within the law enforcement profession.

The internal sections of an organization, small or large, must work together efficiently concerning community policing. Any distrust, law enforcement, or traffic stop issue affecting a section within the organization internally or externally also affects the entire organization and other agencies as well. Such issues can cause a serious change in the behavior of citizens within a community or structure of the organization, creating difficulty for the organization to return to normal in the eyes of the public.

Only police interaction and response to community policing limits the outcome of the results. In most organizations, unity, employee participation, training, functioning policies, community interaction, community meetings, and doctrine suggest being effective. This role promotes a positive outcome in the duties of officers and the type of relationship they will have with the communities that they serve. Community policing and corroboration with the community becomes the points of reference of a team effort and builds commitment by mixing comprehensive management and leadership with all parties involved.

Reflection: Early in my career I had the honor of being heavily involved in many community programs such as The Family Intervention Team, Neighborhood Improvement Team, Community Bridges Program, Adopt a Cop, School Resource Officer, The Roll'RZ Police Band, Fayetteville Police Department TV News, and At-Risk Youth Programs. I even served as a Juvenile Investigator. I learned to embrace the community needs, concerns, and problems early in my career and I saw what the impact could be if good community relations are intact. Chief Ron Hansen was the Police Chief during that time and he was very big on community relations. Chief Hansen emphasized the importance of cops and the community getting along and gaining and retaining the public trust. I remember almost every Thanksgiving Patrol Officers would deliver Thanksgiving meals to families in need. The meals would feed up to ten persons per family. During the Christmas season families were adopted and children would receive toys and bicycles. What an awesome feeling it was to share that love, tears, and trust with the community.

Message Law Enforcement: All the programs and things I mentioned in my reflection were very real and effective during that time and there are agencies today who are doing some or all of these things, but once we as officers break the public trust by displaying negative attitudes, excessive force, racial profiling, and police brutality this unethical behavior takes the front seat in our profession and all that was once good is lost.

Yes I know it may only be a few but that few must be identified and stopped. I know firsthand brother to brother these few bad guys are sometimes noticed amongst their fellow officers, because I have seen it and reported them. Now I am asking you to do the same. We are not going to survive this if the good guys do not stand together.

Message To The Community: 1. Let us continue to love you. 2. Let us continue to serve you. 3. Let us continue to protect you. We need you. **Law enforcement officers all over the world choose to risk their lives every day to do these three things and others.** The pay is low and the probability of getting seriously injured or killed is high but they still want to serve you. I believe together we can stand stronger if we work closer together to identify the right solutions to the problems we are facing. Please know from a man, who has been out here for over 30 years, it is not us against you or you against us.

Chapter Four
Law Enforcement Training

Traffic Stop Training

When Officers go through BLET (Basic Law Enforcement Training) they only receive a minimum 24 hours of traffic stop training that consists of patrol techniques and instructions. In my opinion this is not enough. Agencies must independently devise additional training to ease the challenges we are now facing during traffic stops today.

Today within the law-enforcement profession leaders and officers are faced with many unexpected challenges. Because of these challenges much more training is required. **I would even suggest additional mandatory training statewide that deal with the issues we are facing today.** Amongst the training there is a need for many resources such as technology, software, and information literacy that will enhance their skills and theoretical understanding daily.

Information literacy is defined as recognizing when information is needed, and the ability to locate and evaluate information. For many years like university students, leaders and law enforcement have used the reading and writing method while conducting research. Having the information literacy and technology to do the job effectively is only a small portion of the process. It is imperative that officers and leaders understand what is available through proper training and how to apply it. Use those computers, they won't bite!

The question is what does all this have to do with a traffic stop? Good question. With all the distrust and disconnect law enforcement is facing today, Law enforcement leaders must find and use whatever is available to ensure their safety and the persons involved during a traffic stop encounter. They must find new innovative ways to take away any fears or possible stereotypes.

Information literacy training requires leadership and law enforcement to recognize when resources are needed. In order to be reassured they must locate and evaluate resources and information that contribute to making the right decision. All law enforcement agencies want to produce well-trained and qualified law enforcement officers. This can only be accomplished by leaders in the profession willing to integrate and encourage information and gathering.

Don't try to reinvent the wheel. The wheel is already out there, so go find it. Communicate with other agencies to see what they are doing and how. **Law enforcement officers are not on a heat-seeking mission to hurt, harm, shoot or kill people.** During the basic law-enforcement training academy and annual training new innovative ideas and technology should be readily available such as body camera, and in-car camera systems etc. to allow trainees to become familiar with new possibilities in the field.

Yes I know money and budgeting is an issue but either we pay now or later in a major lawsuit for not being proactive. Most law enforcement vehicles are equipped with MDTs (Mobile Data Terminals). This little patrol car computer can assist with reporting from the patrol vehicle and it gives tons of valuable information about the car or person involved during a traffic stop. Once the information is uploaded the officer may have a little time to see what he or she is dealing with, time to evaluate decision-making, use discretion, and some time to ask for backup if needed.

Technology advances daily and has given leaders in law enforcement the world at their fingertips. Information literacy should start during those trainings to enhance law enforcement officer's research skills early during their career. The law-enforcement profession requires an annual in-service training in order to be proficient. Information literacy should become a part of a yearly in-service training to ensure that officers do not forget important fundamentals that play an intricate part of officer safety, public safety, and the gathering of vital information.

Reflection: When I was a patrolman I made many traffic stops and I wrote many citations for various violations. Some stops became violent, some stops led to drug charges and arrest, and some stops led to verbal or written warnings. Using technology, training, and many other personal skills that contributed to my decision making, I found myself making very good choices during my traffic stops and what was important at the end of the stop and the day is that I felt good about what I did and no one was hurt.

Training coordinator, Sgt. Bob Weathers of the Fayetteville Police Department in Fayetteville North Carolina recruited me in 1987. He always advised officers, once we got home to look over the day and see what we did wrong or right, and what could we do better to ensure our safety and good community relations. With that being said, if I conducted a traffic stop and the driver was kind, polite, apologetic it meant the world to me and by using the technology given to me, if it showed this driver had an awesome driving record, I would use my discretion and not write the ticket. By doing so this often led to good conversation, trust, and confidence in not only me but also my department.

Message To Enforcement: Today officers have so many new tools to do their job more efficiently, but also a window of opportunity to gain so much more. **I am not telling you to give or not give everyone a ticket**, but to combine, the right attitude, technology, good decision-making, and good communication to get the best bang for the buck!

Message To The Community: The one thing I have emphasized many times in this book is having the right attitude and that door swings both ways. Officers are not trained to approach your vehicle with a bad attitude, or to behave in a negative violent manner and you, as the driver should not either. What I am saying is if you see this during a traffic stop or anytime, take the high road, make a mental note, and report this immediately.

Chapter Five
Reasonable Suspicion & Probable Cause to Stop Your Car

To keep it simple, reasonable suspicion is basically a little more than a hunch but less than the proof (probable cause) needed that may give the officer a reason to act when he suspects a crime has been committed or is about to. Probable cause is your actual reason or proof. Among the many questions that I often get from the community (especially drivers) are, "Why did I get stopped? What did I do? Did the officer have a reason to stop me?"

All sorts of thoughts are going through the drivers mind as well as panic and fear. To be honest I have been a cop for over 30 years and I have never been comfortable with getting stopped. In my opinion why you made the stop is something that the officers should tell the driver the moment he or she walks up to the car. When I was hired by the Fayetteville Police Department in 1987 I was trained to tell the driver. **Telling the driver immediately why you stop them can eliminate a lot of stress, tension, nervousness, hesitation, over reacting and most importantly unnecessary confrontation.**

Drivers all over the United States are hearing and being told all sorts of things about cops, police, patrol, 5/0, deputies, etc. Regardless of what the public calls us, we have a lot of scared, unsure, hesitate, drivers of all ages and races. **"The Fear Is Real"** I truly believe everything that they are hearing is over rated but current events have left a lot of doubt and I understand. One major concern for law enforcement is not only ensuring that drivers feel safe and sure when we stop them but also some of our community believes that white cops are out to arrest, shoot, and kill blacks particularly young black boys and black men. I must be honest. In my profession I can honestly say **this is not the focus or goal of law enforcement.** I have personally seen good and bad in jobs, businesses, and careers that include my own. All drivers and parents must educate themselves as much as possible and have many conversations with their young drivers. This is why top leadership, and management are so important. As an Elected Sheriff and a leader of a law enforcement agency I want to believe that all of my officers are doing and going to do the right thing all the time and promote this and I discuss the seriousness of this all the time but my experience has proven otherwise.

Over the years I have terminated officers for racial discrimination, both black and white officers and some situations involved traffic stops. My policy is zero tolerance. During the final interview for employment I reiterate the value of serving the community as a whole and building relationships. I tell my officers when the community sees them they see me, and everything needs to look and be good all the time.

Reflection: When my 20-year-old son Antonio received his driver's license at age 16, I was concerned for many reasons. Safety, speeding, texting, and talking on the phone were some of the few but my largest concern was the traffic stop. Why? Well I'm glad you asked. I sense and see the inconsistencies in today's law enforcement compared to earlier in my career! Okay I said it. I ask myself over and over again as much as his father and mother preached to him on what and what not to do on the road, would he remember what to do during a traffic stop?

I believed, hoped, and prayed that if a cop stopped him his positive actions along with the officer's positive actions would prevent a situation or save his young life, but in the event the officer was a bad seed, my son could rise above it by remembering what he was told to do or not to do. Note: Both parties respectfully doing what they should be doing during the stop equals a positive outcome.

Two weeks after having his driver's license and his first car, I got desperate and had one of my traffic officers stop Antonio coming from school. Yes I did. I had to know if Antonio heard the conversations about what to do and not do if he was stopped by a cop. Lol. I chose the leader of the Hoke County Sheriff's Office Traffic Team Sgt. Michael Murphy, who was viewed as hardcore, tough, non-smiling, and would stop anyone including me. He stopped me three times prior. I gave him my son's route and asked him to stop Antonio to see how he would react during a traffic stop and according to Sgt. Michael Murphy Antonio did every single thing I had told him he should do.

A few days later Antonio realized it may have been a setup and asked me did I have him stopped. I confessed, but I asked him how did he feel when he saw the blue lights? He stated that he was nervous and asked himself what did he do to get stopped by the cop. He further stated that the officer was stern, but very professional.

One thing for sure is that an officer should never ever stop any vehicle without a legitimate reason. This is called reasonable suspicion and probable cause. I have learned over the years that these two words are one in the same and are often used interchangeably. Not to get too technical, when an officer stops your vehicle it does not mean you are under arrest. The stop is considered a non-custodial/seizure. This is for the purpose of upholding the 4th amendment and must be supported by reasonable suspicion and probable cause.

During this non-custodial stop, all passengers may also be detained as well. When an officer makes the determination that a crime or violation has been committed the officer must weigh out the seriousness of his stop and ensure there are sufficient facts to support the stop. Officers are trained over and over again on this. During traffic stops there must always be integrity! Don't fake it to make it! There should be no guessing or assuming.

Message To Law Enforcement: When you stop a vehicle set the stage immediately, because the vehicle is pulling over because you turned the blue light on them. Regardless in a few seconds you will approach the driver. Loud boisterous comments can immediately start a confrontation. Comments like "Do you know why I stopped you?" Do you know how fast you were going?" "What is your hurry?" "Woman you are going to kill somebody" My fellow officers we are not trained to do this and if you encounter someone who does not give a toot about us in the first place and you start out this way its going to be drama on the roadway. Let's not let our personal feelings or emotions take us away from our law enforcement training and professionalism.

Message To The Community: I can't think of any profession that doesn't involve some type of training. When you are stopped by a cop, you are going to see red flags that make you question why or what the officer did or is doing. I ask you to be patient and do as instructed at all times. Sometimes an inexperienced officer will stop you or a rookie who without intent will make some of the most common mistakes. Just remember the drill if you are not pleased or disagree with the outcome. The leaders and managers are always there for you, so please file a complaint if you disagree and give the officer the respect he deserves as he carry out his duties.

Chapter Six
Arrest Search & Seizures (Vehicle Searches)

Once the vehicle stop is made there may be probable cause to either search the vehicle, make an arrest, or both depending on what you as the driver did wrong. If the officer smells marijuana he can request a drug dog to sniff around the vehicle and or search for drugs.

Please note that without Consent, probable cause (PC), or a warrant, an officer cannot and shall not search your vehicle.

In addition to this for the officer's safety, if the officer suspects a weapon he has probable cause to frisk you from head to toe and other person(s) detained. And if necessary the officer can stop a car at gunpoint while attempting to detain someone. Remember, laws may vary from state to state.

USE OF FORCE (Levels of Force)

There have been so many questions about why does an officer do this or do that? Each situation an officer faces can be the same but end differently because of the circumstances involved. Officers are trained to use and understand the equipment they carry on their utility belt and also the levels of force. The one thing I must re-iterate is that officers are trained to use verbal commands in hopes of preventing an altercation that may lead to hands on or the use of less than lethal or lethal weapons.

According to most law enforcement policies, determining the appropriate amount of force to use when confronting a resistive subject can be problematic for the officer. It is certainly a good thing for an officer to resolve a confrontation with verbal direction, however if the situation is at the point where words no longer serve to de-escalate a confrontation then force must be used. Simply stated, officers do not have to exhaust other lower levels of force options before moving to another, so long as it is justified.

The amount of force an officer employs in effecting control or defending himself/herself is generally guided by surrounding circumstances. For example, multiple suspects, surroundings, size of the suspects, etc. Law enforcement officers should use only the amount of force reasonably necessary to accomplish lawful objectives. Law enforcement agencies will not tolerate excessive force used by an officer on any citizen.

The explanation of the limitations of the law upon use of force by an officer will provide them with the necessary knowledge so they may perform their duties confidently and wisely, without subjecting themselves to criminal or civil liability. **In no way does the policies of any law enforcement agency intend to limit the officer's ability to use force, when and if the proper circumstances exist. An officer is**

expected to retain the right to defend himself or others with as much force as is necessary to affect such defense.

Use of Force Justification

A law enforcement officer is justified in using force upon another person who he reasonably believes has committed a criminal offense. Force is also justified if a law enforcement officer is defending himself or a third person from what he reasonably believes to be an imminent use of physical force while attempting to make an arrest, or prevent an escape.

Lethal or Deadly Force

The one question that is common in a lethal or deadly force situation to include traffic stops is why did the officer strike, pull his gun, or shoot a person. This is not something an officer set out to do in any situation. What does lethal and deadly force mean? Lethal or Deadly Force includes, but is not limited to, the use of a firearm or striking a subject with an impact weapon on areas such as the head, neck, clavicle, groin, or multiple strikes to organ areas. Why didn't the officer just fire a warning shot?

North Carolina General Statue 15A-401(d)(2) allows agencies to fire warning shots, however each law enforcement agency use discretion in their policies that relate to fire or not fire a warning shot because warning shots are considered use of deadly force. **An officer may draw his weapon when he has reasonable grounds to suspect that the use of deadly force may be necessary.** The officer need not be under immediate attack, but need only be reasonably apprehensive that a deadly force situation could occur. Policies are intended to allow the officer to have his weapon ready in such circumstances as answering a silent alarm, or confronting a subject when there are reasonable grounds to believe he may be armed, or who may otherwise cause the officer to reasonably fear for his life. A law enforcement **officer may shoot at a moving vehicle if it involves a possible risk of death or serious injury to him or innocent persons.**

Reflection: One of the most common traffic stops I experienced as a patrol officer that led to an arrest, search, and seizure usually involved two to four persons/teens in a vehicle smoking marijuana. In this situation the driver is not aware of his driving violations or actions and does something that gave me reasonable suspicion to stop his vehicle. As I follow the vehicle for a short distance to be sure, probable cause is established and I going blue. As I approached the vehicle I smell a strong odor of marijuana and notice everyone fidgeting. I back off the approach and call for backup and a drug dog/K9. Once all protocols are established, the vehicle is searched and marijuana packets, along with buds, and drug paraphernalia are found. Now it gets tricky. I ask the question. Who does the drugs belong to? No one owns up to the drugs. Of course not, so guess who gets the charge? In this situation I have seen the driver get the charge and in some circumstances I have seen everyone in the car get charged. The unfortunate part is that in most cases mom or dad's vehicle is usually towed. My son and daughters have heard this story over and over again!

A Message To Law Enforcement: When we are out on patrol, we are aware of what the law is and what we can and can't do. We also know our limitations. The average driver has no clue if what we say or do is right, wrong, or illegal. Please do not take advantage of this. Let's not abuse our authority. Let's not use any more force than necessary. **We are not bullies.** Please avoid the stereotypes and be mindful of the fear factor of black male drivers especially black teens. "**The**

Fear is Real". Basically as you patrol don't allow the dreadlocks, hoodies, earrings, neck or facial tattoos, bagging pants, etc. to influence your decision-making and attitude towards a driver during a traffic stop. I've had officers tell me that they are somewhat afraid of blacks. Trust me if you are a law enforcement officer with this problem you might want to rethink your career. I also advised them that understanding culture diversity is a must when it comes to our training today.

A Message To The Community: Please tell your young drivers not to put red flags on the vehicle they are driving. Let's keep it real, it is something about seeing a vehicle day or night with four to five guys riding together and it doesn't matter if the crew is black, white, native American, or Latino. Is it a crime? Absolutely not but it draws attention to any officer on patrol especially late at night and believe it or not there are many situations where this scenario has led to robberies, break-ins, gang violence, and anything else that is not good. Sorry but it does. It is simply not a good look. Encourage your kids not to do this if all possible. **Advise your young drivers to not ride friends around who are packing illegal drugs or weapons.** Most of the time they are driving your vehicle and if it belongs to him, you are probably making the car payment or paying for the insurance. This is very important. My wife and I have preached this to our kids over and over again. Don't do anything that will alert law enforcement or draw attention. Please.

Chapter Seven
Biased Base Profiling (Racial Profiling)

What exactly does biased based profiling mean? What is it? **Throughout the community it is often referred to as racial profiling.** Well in simple definition and in my opinion and others, it is when law enforcement targets a particular person or persons for unethical reasons such as race. This is bad and has been one of the most highly publicized community concerns and complaints today. **North Carolina General Statue 14-110** was established to minimize and stop all law enforcement agencies from biased base profiling in the State of North Carolina.

At the Hoke County Sheriff's Office our policy clearly states we are committed to the highest standard of courtesy and professionalism in all contacts with the public and between employees in the workplace. Bias for or against any person because of race, ethnic background, gender, sexual orientation, religion, economic status, age, cultural group, or other identifiable group is not allowed! **All officers must avoid taking action or using language that is reasonably understood to be derogatory to any such group, or reflects bias for or against any such group during a traffic stop, or any situation.**

Stopping a vehicle or person, issuing a citation, searching a person, or vehicle, making an arrest, or taking any action in traffic contacts, field contacts, seizing assets or initiating the forfeiture of property because of the race, ethnicity, national origin, or any common trait or group characteristics of an individual is absolutely unacceptable! When my officers conduct a traffic stop the following protocol must take place:

A. All Deputies must accurately record all data required by N.C.G.S. 114-10(2A) on the Traffic Stop Report SBI-122 form. Stops to investigate any crime other than a

Chapter 20 (motor vehicle law offense need not be recorded under N.C.G.S. 114-10(2A).

B. Supervisors will place all completed Traffic Stop forms in the designated box in the Uniformed Services Captains office after review.

C. All data will be entered by the 10th day of the following month on all reports submitted by Deputies.

D. All data will be for public viewing, with the exception of officer ID number, at the SBI-DCI website:

http:www.trafficstops.ncsbi.gov

The Traffic Stop Report SBI-122 must be kept on file for three years.

Supervisors must enforce the policies of their law enforcement agency and they must ensure the requirements of N.C.G.S. 114-10(2A) are correctly understood and complied with by Subordinate Deputies. Supervisors must review the SBI-122 forms prepared by subordinate officers, counsel and correct any subordinate Officer concerning any action or language that reasonably indicates bias prohibited by the policy or a violation of the policy, and initiate and document disciplinary action against any officer if counseling does not correct a bias problem.

All citizen complaints alleging bias in action or language must be documented and investigated promptly, thoroughly, and impartially. **Appropriate disciplinary action must be taken and documented to ensure future violations by the same officer will not occur.** In addition to this all supervisors must continually monitor traffic stop data submitted by subordinate officers to be alerted to any pattern or practices suggesting a violation of policy. Closer supervision and counseling may be appropriate in any given case.

The Uniformed Services Captain shall conduct an annual review of the agency practices, including traffic stop data and citizen concerns, to determine if there is any pattern or practice in law enforcement activities by any officer suggesting a violation of this policy. Any abnormal disparities must be investigated to determine if policy is being violated. Appropriate corrective action should be taken in any case of sustained complainant based on biased action or language. Remedial training and counseling may be required of any officer who has engaged in conduct or used language that is reasonably interpreted as violating policy. **A serious intentional violation of policy may result in suspension, demotion, or termination.**

The Hoke County Sheriff's Office and other law enforcement agencies require their officers to successfully complete annual training. **The Hoke County Sheriff's Office is a Nationally Accredited Law Enforcement Agency** and it is our policy to prohibit racial profiling and see the need for ethnic, or cultural diversity, community relations, and professionalism toward the public and in the workplace. In addition training must stress that professionalism, courtesy, and impartiality is the expected norm for all Deputies and employees. **Our agency is Nationally accredited by the Commission on Accreditation for Law Enforcement Agencies.**

Reflection: Several years ago I purchased my first luxury car. It was a shiny royal blue BMW sports coupe. It was nice. It had 30-day tags on it, which made me stick out like a soar thumb or was it something else? One sunny day I drove to a local Burger joint and went through the drive through and ordered my food. As I was waiting for the clerk to hand me my bag, I observed a cop behind me in the drive through line as well. Officers get hungry too and must eat. When the clerk handed me my bag, I slowly pulled off and put my chill back on and leaned a little with excitement about my new ride. As I exited the drive through I heard a loud siren, so I quickly looked in my rearview mirror and there was a blue light. I immediately became concerned because what could I have possibly done wrong buying a whopper? I was still in the parking lot so I pulled safely across two parking spaces.

The white officer walks up to my window with an attitude and screams, "How in the hell can you afford this car?"

"Excuse me?" I said.

"What kind of work do you do? I'm a cop and I don't drive one of these."

I looked at him and his nametag and politely asked, "Why did you stop me?"

Placing his right hand on his gun, his voice became louder and he says, "You need to give me your license and registration."

At this point I realized what this was and before this went any further I stated, "I am a cop as well with the Fayetteville Police Department and my name is Hubert Peterkin. Please allow me to get my credentials from my console."

The officer quickly changes his tune. He says, "You are Peterkin?"

I reply, "Yes I am, and I am asking you again why did you stop me?"

With a smile, the officer says, "Oh we are looking for a car like this and yours fit the description. Sorry for the inconvenience Peterkin. I heard you are doing a good job over there in Fayetteville."

As I was putting my seatbelt back on I told him I personally knew his Chief of Police and asked him how did he think his chief would feel about this stop. The officer immediately turned and walked away. Two days later I filed a formal complaint.

In short, the officer lied about his reasons for stopping me and was later fired for racial profiling.

Message To Law Enforcement: **Please, Please, Please** don't stop a vehicle unless you absolutely have reasonable suspicion and probable cause.

Under no circumstance should you target a person or persons because of their skin color, gender, or for any other reasons listed in this chapter. If you know you have this problem please seek employment elsewhere because it's not acceptable. Remember who you are at all times and your purpose.

Message To The Community: I wish I could tell you that this will never happen to you or your teen drivers. What I can tell you is to always be ready. Be on your guard, but respectfully take a mental note of everything that happens during the vehicle stop to include the officer's name. Don't engage the situation. Avoid a confrontation at all cost. Stay focused and make sure that you know there is a complaint process to assist you if this goes wrong.

Chapter Eight
How to Stop for A Cop (Step by Step)

This is how it all begins. You are driving down the road and all of a sudden you see a blue light and in a few seconds you realize it is you that the cop is trying to stop. You ask yourself the question. Why is this cop stopping me? My advice to you is:

1. Remain calm. Take a deep breath and don't try to analyze yourself or the situation. Do not flee into a police chase or try to avoid the stop or give the appearance you are not going to stop.

2. Immediately turn on your right turn signal and start looking for a safe place to pull over. Try to avoid stopping your vehicle in heavy traffic or in the roadway. This is very important especially for women, seniors, and inexperienced teenage drivers. Do not damage or tear up your car

in a panic to pullover. If it is during the night hours, be extra careful in pulling over off the roadway. The officer expects you to safely pull over.

3. Once you have safely pulled over and stopped, put your car in park, and roll your window down. Please take your foot off the pedals. There will be some circumstances that you will be asked to switch off the engine. This usually happens when a crime has been committed so regardless, please do what the officer asks you.

4. Place your hands on your steering wheel. If it is at night, switch on your interior lights so the officer can get a clear view of your interior. Do not be fidgeting around for papers or other items, under the seat, glove box, and visors. **STAY CALM**. If your license and or registration are in your wallet, purse, or glove box wait until the officer asks for them and advise him where

it is so he may observe your movements. Please. Again roll down your driver side window and wait.

5. Note: As you are pulling over your vehicle the officer is trained to watch and observe your parking and movements. He is probably using his technology to obtain as much knowledge about you, and your vehicle as possible.

6. The officer will also try to position his vehicle to ensure his safety as well. As he exits his vehicle and approaches your vehicle remain calm no matter what. You probably have a million questions but please let the officer speak to you and advise you of why he stopped you and the situation. As the officer approaches your vehicle, Please stay in the car. Don't get out to meet him halfway (Keep your hands empty at all times). Please!! **Now the officer is standing at your window, please don't start cussing, fussing,**

screaming, etc. I am serious. This happens a lot. Secondly please don't have your phone up to your ear talking!! Remember to place your hands where they can be seen, preferably the steering wheel. I have seen drivers place their hands on the dashboard and that's acceptable. For safety reasons the officer needs to see your hands.

7. **At this point the officer should speak (politely) and advise you of why he stopped you** (this is important and in my opinion sets the stage for everything to ensure a positive outcome). **Both parties should be respectful and polite.** If you are not aware of the reason(s) he stopped you, please ask politely.

8. The officer will ask you for your license and registration. As I previously stated, If your license is in your wallet or purse let him know that you need to get them out and if your registration is in the glove box

let him know and allow him to observe you reaching for them.

9. Once the officer has your information he may at that moment give you a verbal warning and leave, or ask you to standby as he walks back to his patrol vehicle to further investigate the stop.

10. As the officer returns back to your vehicle make sure you are in the same position as before.

11. If the officer issues you a citation/ticket he will advise your court date, signatures and explain your options for court and fines with all other details. **Note that signing the ticket does not mean you are admitting guilt.** Signing is acknowledging you have received it.

12. If you disagree please do not try to settle it on the side of the road. File a complaint or make your argument in court.

13. If you wish to make a complaint each law enforcement agency has a complaint

process, which allows you to formally express your concerns. This usually involves top administrative managers.

Reflections: I cannot remember how many traffic stops I made in my career but I do remember the look on the faces of many drivers when I approached their vehicle. **No one wants to get stopped by a cop, not even me, but there is a reason cops are out there.** I have stopped vehicles and had some of the most pleasant times beside the road and made new friends and the stop would end well. There were also times when I would be treated very ugly with disrespect that involved loud yelling and cussing. Either way I hated stopping vehicles.

However, it was part of my job as some unattended traffic violations can cause a lot of serious safety issues that harm or even kill other drivers on the road as they travel. The worst feeling is not seeing a violation and that speeding, drunk, or reckless driver crashes and kills someone. I have seen this many times. In addition officers often stop vehicles on their way to rob, rape, or kill someone and because of their training they save many lives.

Message To Law Enforcement: As we continue to protect and serve our communities let us not forget the dangers involved with traffic stops. If there are ten steps to do it right and safe each time lets not do seven, eight, or nine, because if you do any less, you leave room for errors that can cost you your job, your life, or harm to others. **Leave your attitudes, personal issues, and prejudices at home.** You have an awesome responsibility that requires nothing but the best you have to offer and there is very little room for mistakes especially now. Let's be mindful of all the fears involved of both the driver and you as a law enforcement officer.

Message To The Community: Getting stopped by a cop is always the last thing most people expect as they travel to and from work, movies, church, or to the grocery store, but it happens. The key thing to remember is that at any time without knowing you may have a vehicle issue, a noticeable malfunction, expired plate, tail light out, brake light out, and the list goes on.

If an officer notices these things he is probably going to stop you. The last thing I want you to do is to be afraid of the blue light and the officer. We are not out there to make your day a nightmare. A vehicle stop usually last 20 minutes or less. How both the officer and you as the driver conduct yourselves is key to having a traffic stop without an incident. Both you as the driver and the cop have the responsibility of ensuring a positive outcome.

If you have a weapon in the vehicle you should immediately tell the officer. It does not matter whether you have a gun permit or not, please tell the officer. If you have a permit to carry the weapon, it is probably concealed/hidden in the Glove box, console, under the seat, or in the trunk.

How to Stop for a Cop

Wherever it is let the officer know. If you do not have a permit the weapon should be visible preferably on the seat. Please don't reach for it or try to show or hand it as the officer walks up. Keep your hands on the steering wheel.

Remember my number one rule:

Everyone safely goes home from a traffic stop! "Let's stay alive"

Chapter Nine
How to File a Complaint

The decision to file a complaint may be a tough decision for many drivers during a traffic stop, but it is a must if you feel that you have been wronged, treated unfairly, or you just disagree with the officer's decision. Whatever the case may be, just file the complaint. What happens if you don't file the complaint and you decide to just let it go? You will most likely establish a negative feeling towards cops and you will tell others of your experience and it then spreads and becomes a larger negative throughout the community.

Why?

There are folks who trust and believe in you and they will take your word for it. It is the policy of law enforcement agencies to investigate all complaints of alleged employee misconduct, to equitably determine whether the allegations are valid or not and to take appropriate action. **Please give law enforcement leaders and managers a chance to look into your concerns.** Most law enforcement agencies have a section that handles all investigations including traffic. When you decide to file a complaint making a phone call is only the beginning, so make the call.

Most agencies like the Hoke County Sheriff's Office will want you to come to the office and give a written statement and the complaint is documented on a formal complaint form. Your complaint can usually be accepted by any supervisor to ensure that your concern will not go unheard. It always helps to have an officer's name and or vehicle number, which is usually located in the left or right corner of the rear window or rear bumper.

Most complaint forms like the Hoke County Sheriff's Office will contain the following:

How to Stop for a Cop

1.   Internal control number;

2.   Date occurred;

3.   Date received;

4.   Type of complaint;

5.   Allegation;

6.   Deputy/employee involved;

7.   Complainant;

8.   Supervisor or investigator assigned;

9.   Disposition; and

10.   Date completed.

Please note that all complaints filed will be taken seriously. Any allegations of misconduct by an officer could result in discharge, suspension, demotion, or criminal charges.

Frequently Asked Questions & Answers

QUESTION: What do I do if it is at night and I am not sure it is a real officer with the blue light? **Blue light bandit!**

Answer: Slow your vehicle down. Turn on your caution lights/flashers. Immediately dial 911 and advise the dispatch of your location and tell them, there appears to be an officer trying to stop you and ask dispatch to confirm. Once you receive conformation safely pull over. **If you don't have a phone or phone reception, find a well-lit area or place of business such as a store, gas station etc. Then safely stop your vehicle. Remember the protocols in chapter 8.**

QUESTION: Why does the officer shine his flashlight in my car at night?

Answer: Officers shine their flashlight in vehicles at night during a traffic stop for their safety **and the light should not be put directly in your face.** The officer needs to have a clear view of your vehicle interior.

QUESTION: Why is the officer sitting in the car so long after he stops me?

Answer: During a traffic stop officers use different technologies to perform their duties. During the stop the officer could be in communication with dispatch about you or your vehicle or verifying information. All of this contributes to safety.

QUESTION: What if I have a gun in my car?

Answer: If you have a gun in your vehicle, tell the officers immediately. Do not try to hand it to him or reach for it. Please. **(Refer to chapter 8)**

QUESTION: Why do other police cars pull up when I'm stopped for just a traffic offense?

Answer: During a traffic stop it is not unusual for another officer to pull up to share information or to ensure that the officer is safe during the stop.

QUESTION: What happens if I don't have my license on me?

Answer: Tell the officer that you have a license but not on you. Politely apologize. He can run a check to see if you are in the system. It is his discretion whether he chooses to issue you a ticket.

QUESTION: What do I tell my teenage black son who drives and is afraid to be stopped by cops?

Answer: Please know as a black male officer with a son who drives, that I am aware of the fears that the black community has regarding traffic stops and it is unfortunate, but it is out there and **"The Fear Is Real"**

It is important that young black male drivers know that we as law enforcement officers care for them as much as others and want nothing more than to treat them with the utmost respect and fairness as we do all others.

When a cop stops him or her it is important that there is no confrontation, or disrespect. So many times we are met with confrontation or resistance. I encourage our teens to allow us to do our job and like I stated earlier in this book, follow the protocols for reporting any unfairness or concerns by an officer.

In addition to this I ask parents to help us by advising them to do the same. If there is an officer out that does anything unethical during a traffic stop, sooner or later he will be noticed and stop.

QUESTION: What do I say to my young college driver who has a vehicle on campus, especially the first year?

Answer: One of the scariest things for parents is when their teen takes the car to college. Some advice for our future leaders is not to drink, and definitely don't drink and drive.

There is a lot of fun during the college years. College life is a time to remember. Make good memories. If you go to parties know what you are drinking! As a matter of fact, get your own drink (sodas please!). Do not let someone hand you something to drink not knowing what he or she gave you. A lot of college students get caught off guard and consume drinks that may get them drunk, high, etc.

In addition to this, as you travel to and from, please watch your speed and read the signs because unless you are in a college close to home it is easy to miss the key details that may keep you from making a mistake and getting a ticket for violation.

Please don't text and drive! Minimize your phone activity as much as possible.

If a cop stops you, follow the guidelines and steps listed in chapter eight of this book.

Lastly as you change lanes, give good signals and carefully make your move.

You are our future!

Guys remember my number one rule, and let's stay safe and let's stay alive.

Conclusion

Law-enforcement agencies are needed in our society today to protect our community in many ways such as: public safety, safety awareness, investigating crimes, gang intervention, drug enforcement, courthouse security, jail enforcement, etc. From day to day there are several uniformed officers with different badges on their uniforms and each one of them are wearing a utility belt comprised of various law enforcement tools, both lethal and nonlethal to include a gun. Regardless, each agency is required to carry out and enforce the laws governed by their local, state, or federal jurisdiction.

The primary goal of all law enforcement officers is public safety. Our focus is keeping the community safe and to investigate crimes and violations committed by those persons who have no intentions or care to do what is right. In addition to this law enforcement agencies establish a pledge or mission statement that outlines an overview of who they are and their departmental intentions. The mission statement serves as sort of a promise to the citizens. In short we must not forget the key importance of our mission.

For example:

Mission Statement: Hoke County Sheriff's Office

The Hoke County Sheriff's Office strives to provide the highest level of professionalism possible. Our effectiveness will be measured by the absence of crime in our streets and neighborhoods. Our office will follow the highest set of standards and principles and in doing so our quality of life will greatly be enhanced. Our law enforcement services will be responsive to the needs of our communities; where as the primary goal of the Hoke County Sheriff's Office is to protect life and property.

In doing so we will be responsible for our actions and accountable to the citizens of Hoke County; it is our goal to obtain the highest level of professional ability, with emphasis focused on both individual and organizational integrity.

Our office will implement new and innovative measures and lead Hoke County Sheriff's Office throughout the 21st century by providing professional law enforcement services. We as a united team will accomplish this by carefully managing our financial resources and implementing creativeness, community involvement, and innovative approaches with excellence in order to meet the needs of our citizens.

People often get confused with the uniform, or the type of cars seen when it comes to law enforcement, but understand that in a sense they are all the same with the same goals. Here is the territorial breakdown of their responsibilities. Territorial jurisdiction refers to the assigned areas in which a law enforcement officer is empowered to act. This is a basic overview of the territorial jurisdiction of the below agencies. Officers may have jurisdiction outside their ordinary geographical assigned areas pursuant to mutual aid agreements.

Officers must consult their agency for specific guidance concerning their territorial jurisdiction. Let's take a quick look at the different law enforcement agencies in North Carolina and their different jurisdictions. Regardless of their jurisdictions each agency has the power of arrest and must follow the guidelines of their assigned areas. Through mutual aid agreements officers are allowed to work outside their assigned areas. Below are a list of state and local agencies and responsibilities. Statewide officers have statewide arrest authority.

State Law Enforcement

(1) State Highway Patrol (often referred to State Troopers)

(2) Division of Motor Vehicles/DMV (often referred to as officers, inspectors or agents)

(3) State Bureau of Investigation (SBI Agents)

(4) Alcohol Law Enforcement (ALE Agents)

(5) Wildlife Officers (Enforce all wildlife and hunting laws)

(6) Probation and Parole officers

Local Law Enforcement

(1) The Sheriff is an Elected Official who is elected by the people. He and their deputies have the authority to arrest throughout the county they serve to include the city jurisdiction. Any felony committed within the county gives a Deputy Sheriff the authority to arrest anywhere in the state. When county and city law enforcement join forces the enforcement jurisdiction is mutual.

(2) City police officers have a jurisdiction limit to enforce and make arrest with the exception of one mile from the city line.

(3) Alcohol Beverage Control (ABC) officers are usually employed by county or city and they arrest in jurisdictions that they are employed in, meaning city or county.

(4) Company police officers have the authority to arrest and enforce laws on property owned by

someone. Basically they work for private or business employers.

(5) Campus police officers protect and serve our college campuses.

Hubert A. Peterkin:

The Untold Story &
The Making of An Officer

I have always dreamed of being a cop, but the truth of the matter is, the odds were against me to survive. The early part of my life is what humbled me, challenged me, and sent me on a life journey that I often go back to in my mind to see where God has truly brought me from.

In 1962 I was born to the late Hubert Peterkin and Onnie B. Peterkin in Brooklyn New York. My father never finished high school and my mother only made it to a middle school status. Together they had five children, Mary Bratcher Peterkin (Winkie), Sim Peterkin (Salvador), Sharon Peterkin Bowden (Coo-Coo), and Dennis Peterkin (Bam), and me better known as Spanky. Yes, we all had nicknames at birth.

Growing up in our home with my father was beautiful and we had the best of everything. He was a good provider and protector. Then one day too late, my mother realized that dad had a drug addiction. The drug addiction of my father led to a hostile home environment that consisted of the abuse of my mother. My mom, without an education or job, depended solely on my father and spent many days broken and bruised by his beatings.

Late one night while drunk, my dad seriously assaulted my mom. Afterwards as he was sleeping, she grabbed everything she could pack, emptied our piggy banks and with what little money she had, counted enough coins for all of us to catch a train back home to Raeford North Carolina, where she and my father grew up. Later that next morning I woke up at an old house without running water (pump only), without a bathroom (toilet only), without heat or air (wood stove only), and very limited food or resources.

What I did find were my two wonderful grandparents, the late Joseph and Bessie Melvin. In short my mother never returned to New York. My father eventually returned to Raeford and my mother found herself back and forth in the marriage. Each time the abuse became more intense, sometimes with broken limbs. In fear for her life my Mom eventually had enough and left him for good and my father went back to New York.

The Single Family Home

My mother did the best she could for her children, but was sickly most of the time. She worked at the local Turkey Plant (House of Raeford) for many years and we received Welfare Assistance throughout my high school years. Most of the time there was little or no food at home. The County Welfare Office now known as The Department of Social Services (DSS) provided my mom with a check under one hundred dollars, a box of powder milk, prunes, welfare cheese, and raisins each month. Mom never owned a car or had a driver's license so she walked, bummed a ride, or hitched a cab whenever she had some lose change.

My brother Sim and I would eat at anyone's house that would bless us with a meal. **Thank God for Mother Lucille Cunningham, and Ms. Evelyn Quick Allen for feeding us so many times.** I hated this life and I was embarrassed. Some of the other kids in the neighborhood and at school would laugh and tease my brother Sim and I. We would get bullied at school and as we often walked from the stores with food. Guys would jump us and take my mom's change, break the eggs or smash the bread etc. I think you get the picture.

Most of the time we only had two sets of clothes per week and my mom had to wash them by hand with just water only, because she could not afford to buy washing powder as she called it back then.

It was the same situation with soap. Most of the time there wasn't any soap and yes the teachers spoke to me about this because other kids complained about our odor.

Regardless of the situation I never stopped dreaming about being a cop. I loved the super heroes such as Batman and Superman. I just wanted to save everyone one day and be the good guy.

My mom could only afford the worse homes to rent. These homes were always too small (less than 900 square feet), usually with two bedrooms, hardly large enough to accommodate nine people. Yes I said nine. My mom raised and cared for three of my cousins: Ben Bratcher, Ronnie Melvin, and Robert Melvin. We all grew up as brothers.

The little 13 inch black and white TV we had only played two or three channels as we all huddled around it using a wire clothes hanger as an antenna to help with a signal for reception and pliers to turn the channels. I know what it is like to live with rats, roaches, and bed bugs, because we lived with them all. One particular home that we lived in on Jones Hill had all three, But that was the very best my mom could do.

By the time Sim and I were nine and ten years old we started working in the tobacco and cucumber fields to help put food on the table. Sim and I are eleven months apart in age and Sharon and Dennis are ten months apart. Every Friday we would get paid and give all our money to our mom. She would buy food, clothing, and pay credit. **Stores such as John K's (Home Food), Pete's Grocery, Billy Park's Store, and Jack Tucker's always allowed my mom to get credit because she just didn't have money and she was grateful.**

When mom purchased clothes, it was usually from Family Dollar. There was not a Wal-Mart in the area. **Thank God for my favorite cousin Ms.**

Essie Mae Ray. She often brought us used clothing from people she knew. Most of our clothing were handed down from families who had no further use for them. If the shoes handed down were too small I would squeeze my feet in them anyway or wear the ragged ones even if my toes could be seen. Yes some kids made fun of Sim and I. Today my feet show proof of the pain, and nodules obtained.

Holidays for me were always depressing because of not having food or enough money. My father refused to send money or pay child support for his five children. During Christmas we would set in the house and watch the other children in the neighborhood play with their bicycles and new toys. My mom just could not afford these things most of the time and she would cry so much. She would set us down and talk to us about the true meaning of Christmas and remind us that we were warm and had food on the table that day. We were members of the Freedom Chapel AME Zion

Church in Raeford NC. The church members would often gather food, clothing, and toys for us.

On My Way To Prison At Age 15

In 1975 I was thirteen years old and my father's drug addiction had worsened. On October 29th the day of his 35th birthday daddy jumped out of a window from the 8th floor of a building in Brooklyn New York to his death. I thought my world had ended. Even though he and my mom were apart, I loved him dearly. I could not understand this and I became very bitter and angry at everyone and I hated my life even more.

I became very rebellious and disrespectful towards my mother and my school grades dropped tremendously. The more she tried to manage my temper the worse I became. I talked back to her and even cursed at her sometimes. She eventually felt that she had no alternative but to have me locked away for a year at McCain's Youth Prison. The goal was to seek disciplinary rehabilitation for one year, reevaluate and return home if I improved my behavior.

The Sheriff That Came For Me

As my mother completed the necessary forms needed for lockup I hated her and I thought she was my worst nightmare. I wanted my daddy but he was gone. She restricted me and would hit me with whatever she could and as hard as she could every single time and I deserved it. My Pastor Reverend Melvin from the Freedom Chapel AME Zion Church, Mr. Livingston Lyons, family members and my uncle James Peterkin Sr. begged her not to send me away. Mom hesitated, but sought help in every direction to save me.

One day there was a loud knock at the door and there stood a large white man with a shiny gold badge on his uniform. I later found out that he was Hoke County's Elected Sheriff David Barrington Sr. As I listened from the other room I heard my mom tell him how bad things were with me and she felt that I was a bad influence on my other brothers and sisters. Sheriff Barrington asked, "What does he want to be when he grows up?"

Mom replies, "He thinks he is going to be a cop one day, but with that attitude he is going to end up dead or in your jail."

Sheriff Barrington quickly replies with a chuckle, "Does he really?" The Sheriff then looks at my mom and asked her could he send his deputies by to pick me up and ride me around sometimes.

With a cheerful voice she replied, "I wish you would."

Sheriff Barrington asked, "What is your son's name?"

She said, "We call him Spanky."

As she walked him to the car I can still remember the rage and hopes of going as far away from there as I could even if it meant prison. When my mom came back into the house I heard her tell my sister that the Sheriff isn't going to do nothing. All he wants is a vote.

Two weeks later a deputy car showed up at our home. A tall white deputy comes to the open screen door and asks my mom, "Is Spanky home?"

My mom with much surprise screamed, "Spanky get out here!"

I came to her and the deputy sticks his hand out and says, "Hi my name is Deputy Alex Norton and I come to spend some time with you".

Deputy Norton became the Sheriff after Sheriff Barrington retired. For years Sheriff Barrington kept his word to my mom and sent his deputies to get me. Often times I would walk over a mile to the Sheriff's Office and hang out with the officers.

They always welcomed me. I found myself in the company of my dream and I loved it. It began to change my thinking, and my attitude. I never thought I would sit in the chair of the Sheriff that came for me.

Sheriff Barrington served as Hoke County Sheriff for 26 years and was very instrumental in saving my life. In 1987 he and former Hoke County Commissioner Cleo Bratcher wrote a letter of recommendation to the Fayetteville Police Department asking them to give me my first job as a Police Officer. About 16 years later, In 2002 I decided to run for the office of Sheriff in Hoke County.

As he lay on his deathbed, Retired Sheriff Barrington sent for me. I visited his home on Magnolia St. in Raeford. Sheriff Barrington stated how proud he was of me and he really believed that I would be elected Sheriff. His advice to me was to always treat people right no matter what. He died that year prior to the election.

I eventually realized that I was a blessed young man and God surrounded me with his angels to protect and guide me. Early in age I earned my BA status. Please don't get it twisted. **I am not talking about the Bachelor of Arts that you hang on the wall for all to see. I was Born Again!** I accepted my faith and surrendered. I sought God's favor and advice. It was important to me that I am the best Police Officer that I could be and I took great pride in serving the people. I have learned that the spirit of true love, dedication, and commitment shows in your actions and people can really see it.

As a Law Enforcement officer we are faced with many dangerous situations and officers are killed every day somewhere in this world during traffic stops. **Many families have lost their loved ones in this profession.** I promised myself that I would either die or retire in this job because everything I feel and do comes from my heart. **The path for me to succeed was laid before me**

by so many people and as I often tell young people, "When the opportunity is there for you it is totally your choice."

Everything starts with a dream.

My mother, my first love, did not give up on me. She found the strength and the patience to see me through and I have done nothing but love the hell out of her since. **All the pain, challenges, the suffering, hunger, the cries, and the lack there of, were all part a plan to make an officer who just simply loves and cares for people.**

In 1993, 18 years later, my wife Della and I (prior to marriage) went to my father's grave. I got on my knees and forgave him for everything he had ever done to my mom, the family, and for committing suicide. As I cried, I promised him I would make him proud.

At a very young age daddy told me I would do great things in life and to remember I had the mind to do whatever I chose. He told me that my mind was my own mind no one else's.

Being an Elected Sheriff was never ever in my plan. I never looked at it, or desired it, God did. The Office of the Sheriff is the best job in the world because as the Sheriff so many lives can be affected and touched in so many ways.

Every year my wonderful staff and I bless Hoke County citizens with safety, food, clothing, toys, bicycles, money, and much, much, more. Sound familiar?

So remember one thing, it was not the three degrees I earned that made me, it was the BA status.

About the Author

 Hubert A. Peterkin, the Elected Sheriff of Hoke County located in Raeford North Carolina, is a thirty year highly experienced Law Enforcement leader responsible for managing millions of dollars in the Sheriff's Office and Detention Center's budget. As the Elected Sheriff, Peterkin has a challenging and rewarding position where his management, leadership skills, and prior Law Enforcement experience have been effectively utilized. Sheriff Peterkin has earned a Bachelor of Science Degree in Government and Business, from Liberty University, a Masters of Management and Public Administration from the University of Phoenix. He is also a Doctoral

Candidate for Organizational Leadership & Management.

As a decorated officer, Sheriff Peterkin has been awarded Citizen of the year twice by organizations in his community, Humanitarian Award, Key to the City of Raeford (presented by Raeford's Mayor John K. McNeill), and the Order of the Long Leaf Pine (awarded by North Carolina Governor Pat McCrory), and many other awards.

Sheriff Peterkin is a Singer, Songwriter, Author, Public Speaker, and a consultant. He is married to Mrs. Della Monroe Peterkin and has three children, Antisha Peterkin, LaSwanda Peterkin, and Antonio Peterkin. He is a member of Lewis Chapel Missionary Baptist Church, Led by the Reverend Dr. Christopher Stackhouse Sr.

Sheriff Peterkin served as the President of the North Carolina Sheriff's Association 2015-2016, and he currently serves as the Chairman of the North Carolina Sheriff's Association Executive

Board. **He is available for public and professional speaking engagements.**

For booking, he can be contacted at (910)-670-2601.

Facebook: How To Stop For A Cop

Linkedin: Hubert Peterkin

Twitter: @hokesheriff

YouTube: Hubert Peterkin

Instagram: sheriff_pete

SnapChat: Daddy Pete

GooglePlus: Hubert Peterkin

Website: www.hubertpeterkin.com

Email: lifematters@hubertpeterkin.com

"How To Stop For A Cop" is a product of Hpeterkin & Associates LLC.

Governmental Concerns

National, State, and Local Governmental Concerns For Building Public Trust, and Law Enforcement and Community Relations

In 2015 President Obama formed a Task Force on 21st Century Policing. In the final report 59 recommendations were made. Below are two statements from the Executive Summary:

"Trust between law enforcement agencies and the people they protect and serve is essential in a democracy. It is key to the stability of our communities, the integrity of our criminal justice system, and the safe and effective delivery of policing services."

"Building trust and nurturing legitimacy on both sides of the police/citizen divide is the foundational principle underlying the nature of relations between law enforcement agencies and the communities they serve"

https://cops.usdoj.gov/pdf/taskforce/taskforce_finalreport.pdf

Figure 1 President Obama and Author

North Carolina Governor Roy Cooper has stressed concerns for accountability and rebuilding Law Enforcement and Community relations throughout the State of North Carolina.

Figure 2 Governor Roy Cooper and Author

Figure 3: U.S. Attorney General Eric Holder (Retired), Author, and Governor Roy Cooper

In the State of North Carolina, Hoke County is represented by two men whom have gone above the call of duty as it relates to Law Enforcement and Community Relations, Public Safety and Officer Safety. North Carolina House of Representative Garland Pierce (48th House District) is one of the leaders of the North Carolina

Black Caucus in the North Carolina General Assembly. Representative Pierce has formed initiatives to address Law Enforcement and Community Relations. Ken Goodman (66th House District) was the Primary Sponsor for House Bill 21 that places a list of instructions on what new drivers should do when Law Enforcement stops them.

Figure 4 Rep. Ken Goodman, Author, Rep. Garland Pierce

References

Barsade, S., & Gibson, D. (2007). Why does affect
    matter in organization? *Academy of
    Management Perspectives, 21*(1), 36-57.
    doi:10.5465/AMP.2007.24286163

Hoke County Sheriff's Office. (2008). Biased
    Based Profiling. Retrieved from Hoke
    County Sheriff's Office, Policy Number 02-
    11.

Hoke County Sheriff's Office. (2015). Use of
    Force. Retrieved from Hoke County
    Sheriff's Office, Policy Number 02-06.

Bouffard, J., & Muftić, L. (2007). An examination
    of the outcomes of various components of
    a coordinated community response to
    domestic violence by male offenders.

Journal of Family Violence, 22, 353-366.
doi:10.1007/s10896-007-9086-y

Carmeli, A., Yitzhak-Halevy, M., & Weisberg, J.
(2009). The relationship between
emotional intelligence and psychological
wellbeing. *Journal of Management and
Psychology, 24*(1), 66-78.
doi:10.1108/02683940910922546

Chiaburu, D., & Lim, A. (2008). Manager
trustworthiness or interactional justice?
Predicting organizational citizenship
behaviors. *Journal of Business Ethics, 83,*
453-467. doi:10.1007/s10551-007-9631-
x

Chopra, P. K., & Kanji, G. K. (2010). Emotional
intelligence: A catalyst for inspirational
leadership and management excellence.
*Total Quality Management & Business
Excellence, 21,* 971-1004.
doi:10.1080/14783363.2010.487704

Cooley, J. W. (1972). *Police discretion: Law and equity.* University of Ottawa (Canada)). *ProQuest Dissertations and Theses,* , 226. Retrieved from http://search.proquest.com/docview/85 9468093?accountid=35812

North Carolina Justice Academy. (2016). Arrest, search and seizure/constitutional law. Retrieved from North Carolina Justice Academy, Basic Law Enforcement Training Manual.

North Carolina Justice Academy. (2014). Ethic for professional law enforcement. Retrieved from North Carolina Justice Academy, Basic Law Enforcement Training Manual.

Final report of the president's task force on 21st century policing. (2015). Retrieved from https://cops.usdoj.gov/pdf/taskforce/tas kforce_finalreport.pdf

Goleman, D. (1998). *Working with emotional intelligence.* New York, NY: Bantam Books.

James G. Clawson. (2006). Level Three Leadership: Getting Below the Surface, Third Edition. Retrieved from James G. Clawson, Transformational Leadership and Innovation website.

Kouzes, J. M. (2003). *Business leadership.* San Francisco: Jossey-Bass.

Nonaka, I., & Nishiguchi, T. (Eds.). (2001). *Knowledge emergence: Social, technical, and evolutionary dimensions of knowledge creation.* Oxford, England: Oxford University Press.

Rolls, C. (2007, September 21). Citizens have role to play in reducing crime statistics [Final ed.]. *Cowichan Valley Citizen* [Vancouver Island, British Columbia, Canada], p. 8.

Shooshtarian, Z., Ameli, F., & Lari, M. A. (2013). The effect of labor's emotional intelligence on their job satisfaction, job performance, and commitment. *Iranian Journal of Management Studies, 6*(1), 27-43. Retrieved from http://ijms.ut.ac.ir/pdf_30123_9485b832 34cf5d222a0b3aa2b1a99438.html

Trevino, L. K., Brown, M. & Hartman, L. P. (2003). A qualitative investigation of perceived executive ethical leadership: Perceptions from inside and outside the executive suite. *Human Relations 56*(1), 5–37. doi:10.1177/001872670305600 1448

Yocum, R. (2007). *The moderating effects of narcissism on the relationship between emotional intelligence and leadership effectiveness, moral reasoning and managerial trust.* (Doctoral dissertation).

Retrieved from
http://search.proquest.com/

Butterfly Typeface

Publishing

Contact us for all your
publishing & writing needs!

Iris M Williams
PO Box 56193
Little Rock AR 72215
501-823-0574

the Butterfly Typeface

Made in the USA
Columbia, SC
17 February 2018